T0193677

GRANDPARENTS
RETURNING
—— TO ——
PARENTHOOD

A Parent's Recovery Story from Pain to Peace:
A Supportive Guide for Grandparents Raising
Grandchildren and Parents of Adult Addicts

TABITHA SAGE

BALBOA.PRESS
A DIVISION OF HAY HOUSE

Balboa Press books may be ordered through booksellers or by contacting:

Balboa Press
A Division of Hay House
1663 Liberty Drive
Bloomington, IN 47403
www.balboapress.com
1 (877) 407-4847

Print information available on the last page.

ISBN: 978-1-9822-4522-1 (sc)
ISBN: 978-1-9822-4523-8 (e)

Balboa Press rev. date: 03/18/2020

CONTENTS

PREFACE

In the United States, as of May 2017, 2.7 million grandparents were raising grandchildren (U.S. Census Bureau 2017a). The most common reason for this is substance abuse, which often lends to other reasons such as incarceration, child neglect, child abuse, and so on.

Parenting a second time around, along with losing my adult child to drugs, can be overwhelming to say the least. The reason for this book is to help others by sharing tools I have discovered that shifted my life of pain to a life of peace. My vision is to create inspiration in others to find themselves again and find peace in this unplanned journey. By practicing the tools, I present in this book, shifts took place within me, and life started working for me again.

I have learned a lot through my experience of having an adult child who is an addict. And I have learned so much from raising my grandchildren in my fifties because my daughter is unable as a result of her addiction. The learning came when I allowed myself to be open to transformation. After going back and reading my journal writings from the past six years, starting when it all began, I realized that I have come a long way. The tools I discovered assisted in my healing, and things turned around for me in ways I never imagined.

By implementing what I have discovered, I was able to move from a place of extreme pain to peace. I would like be able to help anyone who is in a situation that feels unbearable and wants to find another way of living. Living lives we are worthy of can get muddled by life's situations. This book details how I got out of the mud and was able to move on. Throughout this book, I will reference many wonderful forefront leaders of the past and present and the techniques I learned from them. These leaders have paved the way with their teachings. I am blessed to have learned from them and am happy to share.

As grandparents raising a second generation, a lot of challenges arise. We are not only trying to provide a safe and secure environment for our grandchildren, but we are dealing with our own emotions … the grief from losing our children to drugs, the absent parents to our grandchildren, and all the problems that go far beyond. However, there is a way to transform all the pain and sorrow into a life of peace and happiness.

Grandchildren bring so many blessings, but when the role changes to caring for them full time, we can feel as though we are left with a full plate and little support. This is a crisis that is not talked about, and resources are limited. Support groups are a great way to both offer and receive support. I found the one through the mental health department in the city where I live. Many offer childcare, which can be a bit of respite. The first time I walked into the support group, I was in shock. I didn't expect there to be so many grandparents in my situation. You hear others' stories and find they are much the same—the same pain, hurts, fears and, misery. It feels as if you have joined hands with a very special group of people who are going through it with you. There are also many online support groups available.

My roller coaster was filled with shame, fear, anger, betrayal, and disappointments. I remember holding my daughter in my arms when she was born. There was this overwhelming feeling of love for my first child. I remember having so many hopes and dreams for her. As she grew older, I was proud of who she was becoming. She was creative and smart (did well academically and socially); was involved in sports and a member of clubs, including a young Christian group; and worked two or three jobs as soon as she was of age. She was ambitious and actually bought a brand-new car off the lot all on her own. She worked as a makeup artist and was always buying high-end clothes, shoes, and handbags. Her looks were important to her, and she appeared to have a high self-esteem. I never would have thought someone with such a strong personality and who was so family orientated would become a prisoner to drugs.

When I first found out it was drugs, I had so much anxiety and fear. I didn't know how to help. I was always walking on eggshells, fearing I would say or do the wrong thing. There was a sense of betrayal wondering why and how she could have abandoned her family—especially her children. Her and I had always been so close, and with her first child in the beginning, she was a wonderful mom to him. They had truly bonded. It just didn't seem possible.

There was this shame I felt for her because she didn't love herself. How did that happen? It's shameful when a person would rather be numb, live on the streets, steal, and sell her body instead of being present and wanting to parent such wonderful, loving children.

I would have to say the anger has been one of the hardest of all the things to overcome. The anger was tied to so many things. Much of our family was affected by this because she was an important part of our large family. Lives had been changed or had to be altered because of her and her choices. I was constantly angry. I had to pick up the pieces and change my life for someone else's doing. I was angry my grandchildren didn't have parents who were present. I was angry this person who is the father of my grandchildren had so much control over my daughter and was the driving force to all of this. It felt unfair, and the anger was eating me away.

In the beginning, there was also a lot of guilt as we wondered what we did wrong as parents. What did we miss that caused this? Of course, there is also the addict constantly throwing blame, so that doesn't help. The guilt, second-guessing, and trying to understand and figure it all out was tormenting.

One of the biggest challenges in life is raising children. My work didn't stop when my daughter turned eighteen or when she moved away from home. She is my daughter who came from my womb, and I will always want the best for her. It's hard to witness when she chooses drugs over life. I have found that even with the best parenting, drugs do not discriminate. This type of disaster enters a family and leaves many casualties.

Going through this experience has turned out to be my biggest challenge with the most valuable lessons in my life. Life will often give you whatever is most helpful for your evolution. Viewing life in this manner changes the question, "Why is this happening to me?" to, "What can I learn from this?" I now trust I needed these lessons in order to find my true essence.

My life had been turned upside down. It really was like a roller coaster—the ups and downs, the knots in my stomach and body going into fight-or-flight response. I would jump every time the phone rang or I heard a siren, and even while I was sleeping, my heart was racing. I had to find a way to stop the suffering. It took making it a priority to care for myself. I was especially motivated knowing I had to be all I could be, not only for myself but for the grandchildren.

Life is hard, no doubt. It's all about how we react. That alone can make a big difference. We can cause a lot of suffering to ourselves without awareness and being unconscious. Our mindsets can bring great suffering. I am not an expert by any means. What I share in this book are strategies that have transformed me, and my hope is the information will help you as well.

I have learned to not allow my situation to define me and control my life. For many years, I was managing to be just okay, I was stagnant, waiting for something to happen—for anything to happen to make me love life or even just like it. I would put a smile on my face, but inside, I was miserable. There was a dark cloud that permeated throughout our household. In my desperation of trying to find relief, I started to write my thoughts and feelings down in a notebook. Not only did it validate what I was feeling, but it gave me some clarity. The more I journaled, the more I opened up to other forms of healing. All of this brought me from victim to survivor mode and beyond.

I had to learn and relearn some things and change my thoughts about a lot of things—especially those things I had been conditioned to believe by society. It takes some time to train the mind. It doesn't simply happen because you decide. It takes being aware, taking action, and being dedicated. Like any habit you want to form or give up, it takes time and devotion.

At some point, I knew I needed to change in order for things to change. It was upsetting to me because this wasn't my doing. I questioned why I was the one who had to change. However, it is true. The only thing I have control over is me. This goes the same for forgiving and letting go of anger, guilt, or whatever else was keeping me stuck and unhappy. Those things were my responsibility.

On some level, I used to think I had every right to be angry. The anger was like a time bomb waiting to go off, and it did many times. Sure, anger is a natural reaction, but continuing to live daily with this anger served no positive outcome. I came to realize I had every right to be at peace. So, that is what I chose. Even though I felt I had been done wrong, my grandchildren had also been done wrong, and all the hurt other loved ones had to endure felt unforgivable. It just wasn't worth continuing this way. It wasn't until I decided I'd had enough suffering and implemented changes that things began to shift and new way emerged.

I am important, and my peace is important, so I started acting that way. The mental and physical health of my grandchildren is important, and that is where my focused shifted. Once I surrendered to what is, it didn't matter anymore if I was right or if I felt the absent parents didn't deserve forgiveness, etc. What really mattered was being free from the nightmarish situation that was dictating my life.

We don't have control over life events, but there is a lot we can do with the control we do have. I started to take control over the things I could, like what I think about, how I react, and what is truly my responsibility. The mind is very powerful. You can train it to be your friend or your enemy; you get to decide. When I made the choice that my happiness had nothing to do with another individual or anything external, the turmoil began to subside. A lot of my thoughts that were keeping me stuck changed. I stopped going over and over the past and stopped trying to predict the future. It is futile.

We live in a society where we are constantly told we need external things, people, money, and stuff in order to be happy. We are conditioned to think that things need to be a certain way or we have to be like everybody else, or else something is wrong with us. When I really came to grips with the fact that I am the only one responsible for my happiness, nobody else is, and everything external is fleeting, it only made sense to switch the emphasis from the external to the internal.

We all come into this world for a reason. Truly, there are no accidents. Along the way, we make decisions that take us on or off our paths. My daughter has her path, and I have mine. Once I separated the two and placed my attention on my life and my path, it created a sense of peace. The pressure of trying to figure out my daughter's next moves was gone. I stopped thinking I knew what was best for her and accepted things as there are.

As I have grown in my new ways, I care less about what others think and how things are supposed to be. I am learning more and more not to take things personally. People can keep their stuff, and I will keep mine. I now refrain from thinking of the past; it's over. The past honestly has no use. I stopped wondering what will happen in the future. I try to stay in the present and take pleasure in the now.

Sending love and many blessings to those who read this.
Tabitha Sage

ACKNOWLEDGMENTS

To my wonderful parents who have supported me in everything I do throughout my entire life with the unconditional love of a mother and father.

To my husband, my adult son, my three little ones, and my granddaughter, I love you. To all my family who show up for me and for my children with consistently giving us so much love and support. We are so fortunate to have you all. You all know who you are! I appreciate every one of you.

To Amy, may you find sobriety and peace. I am always sending you love and healing.

Of course, to all the grandparents who are raising their grands and giving of themselves to make for a better future for all.

God bless those parents of adult addicts.

INTRODUCTION

This book is intended to help those who want to find peace and happiness when it seems impossible. The one person you have to live with is yourself. Therefore, practicing the tools in this book will assist you in finding yourself. Taking action will bring about happiness and peace. The tools set forth are not new and, in fact, have been around for centuries, and today we have research and science to back them up. It is a matter of practicing the tools until they become habit. Then shifts will occur. You will discover your true essence. Peace will follow despite circumstances.

In chapter one, I tell my story in chronological order. It starts when my life was thrown an unexpected curveball. I tell a lot of details, but there was too much to include it all. I felt it was important to give some background. I have a feeling my story will mimic the stories of many who read this. Parents of adult addicts tend to go through similar things and find themselves asking, "What next?" The second chapter is about the major shifts that occurred within me. This is what happened to me after I hit what I call my rock bottom and went on a self-discovery trip. I share three tools in the third chapter that I have discovered for healing. I share how by implementing these tools, I found peace and happiness. These tools are also ones that can be used with children to give them some relief in their unplanned journeys. The last chapter concludes by telling how abandoning old ways of thinking and doing brought a new set of guidelines to live by. The journey is not the destination, and so it continues.

Some things in this book have been altered, and the names have been changed to protect the privacy others. Either way, I share my honest feelings and what I know to find peace and happiness when it doesn't seem possible.

My hope is that those who read this will discover they don't need to be victims of circumstances or relationships and/or trapped in painful emotions. Regardless of the external, we can rid ourselves of things that have enslaved us and create the lives of peace and happiness we were intended to have.

Tabby

CHAPTER ONE

ROCK BOTTOM: MY STORY

· · · · · · · · · · · · · · · · · · ·

We often hear how addicts must reach their own rock bottom before they will seek treatment. This rock bottom is different for everyone. In a sense, I can relate to this. For many years, I was suffering. I had anxiety, which sometimes took weeks to overcome. I was constantly sick. For about a year, I literally threw up every day. I was depressed. I hated life. I would cry every day. I hated how my life was unfolding. It was nothing I had imagined or wanted it to be. My mind was repetitively going a hundred miles an hour about how miserable I was and how much life sucked. I was either going over and over the past in my head or imagining all these future scenarios. I was rehashing and thinking about what would have happened had I done this or that differently. I was constantly asking why and how this happened. I was reacting without thinking. I felt defensive and on the edge. I was in an impossible situation. I was trapped.

I was at the mercy of my daughter; as long as my daughter was involved with drugs, I couldn't be happy. I couldn't accept it. It was unacceptable. I wanted something to change, but it felt hopeless, and I felt helpless. I thought if my daughter stopped using drugs, things could go back to normal, and I would be happy and at peace. So, I was in limbo for a long time. I was waiting for something to happen. What? I don't know. I just wanted something to happen that would change the nightmare I was living. My life was consumed with worry, wondering, sorrow, hate, and frustration. I often thought, *Is this it? Is this the life I am stuck with?* Those thoughts made me horribly unhappy. After many years of misery, I finally hit my rock bottom. I didn't want to live that way anymore. I was tired of living in the cycle of expectations and pain, being disappointed, and feeling like a prisoner to life's circumstances. I came to a point where I'd had enough suffering and was willing to do whatever it took to change that.

Most of the time while my two adult children were growing up, I had been a stay-at-home mom. I didn't have a career per se. I don't have a retirement or really much that most people my age have. I had thought it was worth the sacrifice to be home with my children. I worked hard doing as much as I could to give my children well-rounded childhoods. Their father was a good example of a loyal family man and hardworking dad. He too had to sacrifice by working overtime to allow for me to be at home with them.

My daughter, Amy, my firstborn, was a fun-loving person. She had a big heart and was compassionate and thoughtful. She loved family. She was a natural with children. She loved her little brother so much, and it showed. She was always teaching him things and was very protective of him. She loved her little cousins, always wanting to hold them and love up on them. She had a good sense of humor and was really funny. She had a quirky innocence about her. She and I were always very close and did a lot of things together. We would cook, go shopping, go out for sushi, and watch weekly shows and movies together. We had this thing where we collected Jennifer Aniston movies and would binge-watch them. We were always crafting and baking together. She was also a strong swimmer and was on the swim team. She was always into reading, and after graduating high school, she attended a yoga school where she received her certificate to teach yoga. Like most parents in this type of situation, we miss the way our child was before drugs.

AND SO IT BEGINS ...

From the beginning, when my daughter met Scott, she displayed a behavior that was negative and nothing like her. The change was immediate. He was an alcoholic and a heavy smoker. He was divorced, had children, and couldn't hold a job. Amy had never rebelled as a teenager, so I thought maybe this was her rebellion time. I remember thinking, *This has to be a phase.* Amy was too strong of a person. She had goals, so it couldn't last for long.

The first year Amy and Scott were together, there would be weeks and even months when we had no communication. I missed her a lot during that time, and it was hard to understand what was going on.

She lost her concern for her family. She acted and even looked different. When we did talk, many of those times, we would end up having big fights. It made no sense. I couldn't figure it out. I cried every day for that first year because I missed my daughter. I was sad without her and couldn't understand what was going on or how I could change it. It created a lot of pain inside me. During that time, family members reached out to her. No one wanted to give up on her. They all eventually stopped trying because she would not reply. She was only giving to one person—Scott; this included leaving herself out of the equation. He had an unexplainable hold on her. She even seemed frightened of him at times. Yet, he was all she was concerned about. Nothing I tried worked with her; in fact, things got progressively worse. Her lack of respect left me feeling so unloved. She would bash me and accuse me of wanting pity and making it about me. She would throw everything her father or I ever did wrong in our faces. She would put us down continually. She blamed her father and me for things that made no sense at all. I was constantly offended. It was so hurtful.

After about a year and half, my son and I moved to Florida for a year. We applied to school out there so he could work on his bachelor's, and I could work on my master's degree. I couldn't be in the same house with so many memories. I couldn't even be in the same state or city. I was in deep mourning. I knew there was little to nothing I could do, and this made me extremely sad. I wanted to run away, so I did.

I was searching, wishing, wanting for something—anything—because the pain was unbearable. I couldn't see straight. I had suicidal thoughts. I wanted to fill the void and take away the pain. I was in a dark tunnel. I just didn't know what to do or how to be. It didn't feel like this was really happening, but it was. I was so taken by it. Mentally, I was a mess. I just wanted things to go back to normal.

AMID THE CHAOS

Not long after we moved to Florida, Amy became pregnant. She told me that she gave Scott the ultimatum to go to AA and quit smoking cigarettes because the baby was coming, or she would leave him. He went to AA and quit smoking. Then for a little while things seemed to have calmed down. But it wasn't long before Scott returned to his old ways, and she didn't leave him.

We returned from Florida, and my first grandson was born. He was such a joy and a nice distraction from all the chaos. However, before too long, the darkness appeared again. The weird vibes came back, as well as that feeling she didn't like us—her family. It felt like we had some kind of disease. She did everything to avoid us. She was short and rude with us. Something always felt wrong; I just could never figure it out. I struggled with a lot of guilt, low self-esteem, anger, bitterness, and frustration. I felt so unappreciated. As parents, these are things we struggle with anyway. When things go horribly wrong, you question everything and blame yourself.

When my grandson was two, Amy became pregnant with my granddaughter. Things only got stranger. They were always moving (five or six times within a couple of years), and of course, they always had a really good reason for moving. You know, it was the landlord's fault, there were bugs in the apartment, and so on. For a long time, I thought it was relationship problems. For that reason, I tried to watch my p's and q's; I didn't want to get involved in relationship issues. I would give my opinion or advice from time to time, but it fell on deaf ears.

Again, I honestly thought it wouldn't be long before she would get tired of him and leave. She looked skinny, tired, and withdrawn. From what I had known of her at that point, she was not one to take a lot of BS. I kept thinking, *Any time ... It's just a matter of time.*

As time moved along, I saw my daughter become more and more unhappy, but she never communicated clearly. She spoke in riddles. Scott's boys would visit every weekend. I know this was hard on Amy because Scott would put her down about any type of rules she set when the boys were visiting. He would allow the boys to eat and drink things that are not good for children; he would let them stay up until all hours of the night; he would smoke right next to them; he would allow them to go to the playground across the street alone or to the hot tub in another part of the complex alone. When my daughter would say anything, he would be mentally abusive and disregard her. He was not only mentally abusive, but also physically abusive.

IT ALL STARTS TO SPILL OUT

One night, Amy called my mother who is in her seventies and told her she was addicted to pain pills. This is when I first found out it was drugs. She told my mom that she was afraid to tell me and that she needed help. When she did finally tell me, she also said she had started going to NA meetings and was committed to getting past this. So, I thought, *Okay, this must be it.* I didn't understand the severity of the situation or how harmful prescription drugs are. I didn't think it would be that hard to get off of them. She ended up telling me that her friend's dad was the one who had been providing the opiate pills (at twenty dollars a pill) to her and Scott for the last two years. *Wow! Two years?!* I thought. I was pretty stunned. However, I was even more stunned that a grown man with children of his own was providing prescription drugs to others for money. That still stuns me as I write this. She promised to not only attend NA meetings but to get into counseling. That lasted about a month, if that.

When my grandson was three, he came over for a sleepover. This was the first time I noticed a change in him. He was once a happy, carefree boy with a spoiled air about him. He now had worry on his face. He confided in me, with this concerned voice. He said that his baby sister couldn't walk; she was stumbling around and bumping into things, and they had to take her to the hospital. He was starting to take on worries of an adult. I was trying to put it all together. I had already been conditioned to walk on eggshells and watch every word I said to Amy. What was this three-year-old boy saying to me? How should I respond?

Finally, I asked Amy. She explained she had taken my granddaughter to urgent care, and it turned out to be an ear infection. Later, I found out that the poor baby had overdosed on cough medicine. Cough medicine was a nightly ritual of Scott's to help him sleep. On many occasions, I would walk into their house and find opened bottles of cough medicine all within the children's reach. I would close the bottles and put them up high. I noticed Scott's sloppiness was becoming a part of Amy's character. She was becoming more and more like him. It was frightening.

Three months later, I received a call from a friend of Amy's saying that Scott left Amy and took the kids to another state to be with his ex-wife, the mother of his two boys. She said Amy was depressed and alone at her condo. Of course, I immediately went over. She answered the door with a towel wrapped around her looking like a malnutrition ghost. As we spoke, I noticed she had no urgency to get the kids back. She was more concerned about losing Scott than about the kids and their safety. I was so fired up. I couldn't believe what I was seeing or hearing.

I called the sheriff's department to report the kids missing and seek advice on what action to take while she sat there. It was odd behavior, but I didn't know what to do with those feelings. So, I took over and started doing what she should have been doing to try and get the kids back. We headed to the courthouse and filed a child abduction report. Then, I hired a lawyer that cost three thousand dollars that we did not have. We actually had to borrow the money because getting the kids back as soon as possible before they were harmed was top priority to my husband and me.

After a couple of weeks, I was in the shower, and when I came out, Amy was gone. I looked on the wall where we keep the car keys hanging, and the keys to our new car (it wasn't even insured yet) were gone. She ended up being gone for hours. When she returned, said she had been at the courthouse with Scott dropping the abduction charges because he insisted. Again, the hold he had on her was baffling.

After a month of knowing very little about the kids' well-being, Scott decided to bring them back to their condo. My daughter-in-law took Amy over to their condo to see and get the kids. She said it was the weirdest thing because Amy hugged Scott first instead of the kids and was more excited to see him. Eventually, Amy stayed, and my daughter-in-law returned alone. He had kicked my daughter-in-law out and made Amy stay. It was truly unbelievable.

It wasn't long after that when Amy and the kids went to Scott's ex-wife's home in another state a few hours away. I had no idea what this was about. It was just more off-the-wall behavior. She no longer had a cell phone, so I had no way of reaching her. I would get calls from her friends telling me that Scott and the kids were with the ex-wife at her apartment, while Amy was in a hotel or wandering the streets. One of her friends called and said that Scott took Amy's shoes away, so she couldn't go anywhere and that she was all doped up on the streets. Hearing this upset her father so much. I thought he might even have a heart attack. He ended up making the four-hour drive to see if he could possibly find her. But as you can imagine, this was a large task. He never found her.

Another month went by when the four of them finally returned back to their condo to gather their stuff. They had been evicted. They put all their stuff in storage and went homeless. I did not know this until later on. Amy told me some lie about Scott getting a job that would include housing, and until the housing was available, they would be in a hotel. I didn't believe it, but I pretended as if I did. The next few months Amy would drop off the kids to me every Friday through Monday. That was the original agreement, but often, she would show up one or two days later with a million excuses. I had made this agreement with her because I wanted to make sure the kids were safe, if only for those days while with us. I wanted to believe Amy and Scott would use this time to find a way to get out of the mess they were living. I never imagined they would neglect or abandoned the kids. But they did.

My grandson who was four at the time would come in and tell me things that were alarming. One time he said they went camping and that his parents told him to make believe his name was different, so they called him by this different name. Another time he told me that Mommy and Daddy left him and his sister (age two at the time) strapped in their car seats for a long time while they were in some house. Then he asked me, "Grandma, are kids supposed to sleep in the car at night?" My granddaughter would continually have severe diaper rash. It was raw and hard to even wipe her because she would cry in pain. I would ask my daughter about these things, but of course, she would deny it all or have some excuse.

Over the next two or three months, they were sleeping in their car and in and out of hotels. There were a couple of times when Scott called and asked me if I could go get the kids because they'd been kicked out of the hotel. Amy called me crying at least three times saying Scott had been arrested for driving violations. I pleaded with her to let me help her, but she always had some reason and wouldn't take me up on it. I ended up quitting my job because I felt I had to be more available. I was finding that I couldn't trust my daughter anymore. I was in a corner.

As I saw the time coming closer for my grandson to register for kindergarten, I offered for Amy to use our address and register him at the nearby elementary school. I even offered to take him to and from school every day. I would do and say anything I thought would help, but it never made an impact. She never registered him for kindergarten and missed out on the entire school year. When his birthday came and there was no celebration until he came to our house and we had a little party for him, he kept saying it wasn't his birthday. He was so confused. They forgot their own child's birthday! It was hard to wrap my head around it all.

When Halloween came, I planned with Amy to bring the kids over, and we would trick-or-treat in our neighborhood. They never showed up. Later, she told me they drove by my house but didn't come in because they were too high. So, the kids missed out, and they were driving around high with them. *Ugh!*

Most of that November after that Halloween, I lost contact because Amy's phone was disconnected again. I didn't know what to do or think. I couldn't sleep. I would keep my phone by me and would jump every time it rang. I was checking it constantly to make sure I didn't miss her call. I would write her emails, texts, and messages on Facebook, trying to find out if the kids were okay. I was buying Christmas gifts for the kids but wasn't even sure I would see them. It wasn't until a week before Christmas that she called me. She and Scott had been arrested for shoplifting. She was released, but he wasn't because of warrants he had. She asked me to pick her up and take her to her car. When I saw her, I was in shock to see how skinny she was. She looked sickly and dirty. *The kids! Where were the kids?* She told me Scott's brother (who lived in another state) had been watching them since the day after Halloween. *What?* I thought. *She didn't spend Thanksgiving with her kids?* She went on to say that she would come to my house to clean up and eat something, but she never showed up.

THE HOLIDAYS

On Christmas Eve, she showed up at the front door and told me she needed help. She said she'd just taken her last hit and would be going through withdrawals soon. I was mortified. I had no idea what to do. I started to google recovery treatment centers, what to do when someone is withdrawing, and anything else I could think of. I didn't know what to expect or how I could help. I was in a panic. I had waited and wanted this day to come when she would ask for help, yet I was totally unprepared. Recovery and treatment centers cost thousands of dollars, so that was out of the question. I ended up finding an addiction counselor she could see, and her dad took a month off from work and took her every day to NA meetings. I bought a bunch of supplements to assist with the withdrawals and made appointments for her to get a massage and a facial, get her hair cut, and see a chiropractor. This is all we knew to do.

The withdrawals were not easy. She was lethargic and depressed and could barely function. She experienced paranoia, hallucinations, and anxiety and went from sleeping long periods of time to having insomnia. She would stuff food down her mouth and then vomit. It was hard to relax or sleep because she would do odd things. She would smoke cigarettes in the bedroom even though I asked her not to. One time she fell asleep with the cigarette butt burning onto her chest. She would tell me she couldn't think without Scott. Again, it was the strangest thing to see the obsession she had with him. The kids had been out of her care for two months, and still, there was no urgency on her part to get them back. All she thought about was Scott. As the days went by, she started to come back alive. I honestly was thankful that Scott was in jail and she was having that time to heal. Was this it? Was this her rock bottom?

After about two weeks of withdrawing, she went to see the addiction counselor. She was only in the appointment a few minutes when she came out. She said the counselor wanted her to go to urgent care because she couldn't continue with the appointment due to the severe body pain Amy was experiencing. We took her to urgent care, and this was when we found out she was pregnant with baby number three. This news was heartbreaking to me. What was this poor baby going through in her womb? It was terrifying to think about. I went into mom mode, shook it off, and started to try to fix it all. I changed the focus to doing what was best for this new unborn baby. Now, it was about buying prenatal vitamins, trying to ween her from cigarettes, and getting some healthy, well-balanced meals in her.

Scott's brother finally brought the kids to us soon after New Year's Eve, and we celebrated a late Christmas with the children. Everything was on the mend—or so I thought.

Soon after the kids arrived, Scott was released from jail. We didn't allow him to stay in our home overnight. I was not only being cautious because of their sobriety being so fresh but also because my son and my daughter-in-law were living with us at the time. We tried to be supportive in other ways. We paid for a hotel room a couple of times so they could all spend the evening together as a family. We gave them both rides to church and NA meetings. And during the day, we welcomed Scott to visit with the children at our house. However, it wasn't long though before Scott was back to what he does best. He did everything to manipulate the situation and get back into my daughter's head. Anything he said to her, she believed and followed suit.

We truly wanted to help. The problem was that we never knew quite how. It was like trying to find something in the dark. We wanted so bad for both of them to not only get clean for themselves but for their children. This was bigger than all of us. While Scott was at our house, he would ask to use our computer to apply for jobs. Neither of them had a valid driver's license, and their car was not insured or registered. He said he was working on those things. Again, this was another lie.

Months later, I went to make copies of some documents, and when I lifted up the glass to the scanner, there was a copy of a temporary license plate. I looked at the history on the computer, and it was taken from a site that makes fake temporary license plates. There was also a big, black marker sitting on the desk that he'd used to fill in the expiration date. That was his way of working on things—always trying to beat the system.

THIS IS IT

One night, Amy put the kids to bed and told me she was going to look for jobs on the computer. I was so tired that I thought it was a good night to get some sleep. When I was in bed sleeping, I was awakened to my granddaughter crying. I didn't get up right away. I was giving Amy the chance to parent since she had spent months without her children and needed to start parenting again. The crying wouldn't stop, so I finally got up and found she had fallen off the bed. I searched the house for my daughter and could not find her. She didn't have a cell phone, but we had bought a prepaid cell phone for Scott so they could communicate. I called the phone and found out she was with him. She said they were outside talking, and she would be in soon. An hour later, I called again and said I wanted to go to bed, and I didn't want to leave the door unlocked. She was saying she wanted to come back, but he was yelling in the background saying she couldn't come back. She didn't.

For the next couple of days, Amy was not allowed to talk to me per Scott. He would call and harass us, wanting the kids. I was so afraid to let the kids go because I couldn't trust them anymore. I also worried about the vehicle they were driving because the tires were bald. Both Scott and Amy were on drugs, and they wanted the kids. I kept making excuses to not let the kids go, but it only provoked Scott's anger.

One afternoon, I happened to be standing by the front door when I saw the doorknob being turned from the outside. He was trying to open it. He then walked around the house to the backyard and tried the patio door. Thank goodness the doors were all locked. Later, a neighbor said she saw him on the roof, so I think he was trying the upstairs windows. I had so much adrenaline, and not knowing where to turn, I called the sheriff's department and asked for advice. The officer advised that we go first thing Monday morning to the courthouse and file for temporary custody. He said we must turn the kids over to Amy and Scott because they were threatening to accuse us of kidnapping. So, that's what we did.

I remember that day so clearly when we had to turn the kids over to them … They were so little. My granddaughter was still in diapers and using a bottle. I packed a bag for them with warm clothes, and Amy's dad got a cooler together with milk and food for the kids. I got on my knees to be at their level, so I could tell them how much I love them. I told my grandson I'd written our phone number on the inside of his shoe. I said it was our little secret, and it was there if he needed me. They were two and four. My son and daughter-in-law where loving up on them too until the time came for them to leave, and the doorbell rang. A cop came to the door to get them. My daughter sat in her car, and Scott walked up the driveway to the porch to get them. We asked the police officer to check their car registration and insurance and to see if they had valid driver's licenses, and he assured us he had done that. This could not be true because there would be no way for this to be accomplished in two days over the weekend. We had no other choice but to say goodbye to my precious grandbabies.

NEVER THOUGHT THIS WOULD HAPPEN

On Monday, we headed to the courthouse to file for temporary custody. Little did we know that the drive to the courthouse would become a regular drive during the next couple of years. It was always a solemn drive. I never really believed that my daughter would lose her parental rights. I would have bet a lot of money because losing her kids was not her—the real her. I never thought my once strong-willed daughter would be addicted to drugs and a man. She was choosing drugs and a man. I had no choice. I had to find a way to protect my grandchildren. By the way, it turns out there is such a thing as being addicted to another person, and brainwashing is a real thing. She was suffering from a triple whammy. She was in deep.

Not too long after that first court appearance, the judge awarded us temporary custody. However, now the children were in a different state. They had gone to Nevada to live with Scotts mother. Yup! They traveled while being high, with bald tires, no insurance, no driver's license, and no vehicle registration—all with two small children.

Three or four weeks after they arrived in Nevada, CPS (Child Protective Services) did a well check on the children. A couple hours after making the well check, CPS called to inform me that it did not go well. The authorities told me that Scott's eyes were darting back and forth. Apparently, he threw himself on the floor, and while rolling around on the floor, some meth and a meth pipe fell out of his pocket. My daughter was in a second-floor bedroom trying to escape out a window with the children. Scott ended up being arrested, and CPS in Nevada took the children into custody. The next morning CPS flew the children out to me.

When the kids arrived, they were distraught. It was difficult to observe. I didn't ask them a lot of questions because I felt they had been through enough. I figured it would come out if it needed to. I also made sure there was no bad talking or even talking about the parents in front of them. I wanted to be gentle and careful with them. I wanted them to heal.

I really wanted to be a grandma and for my daughter to be a mother. Her actions or lack of actions kept proving more and more that this was not going to happen. Both her and Scott were given a lot of chances as biological parents. The law is very forgiving to bio-parents. In the beginning, they were given the opportunity to have supervised phone calls with the children. They missed ten out of thirteen calls when the state finally dismissed the opportunity from them. The kids would wait and wait for the call to take place until the eldest decided he didn't even want to talk to them anymore. When it was my granddaughter's birthday, they arranged to call her on her birthday. Yet, there was no call. It was a simple phone call. That is all they had to do, and they still couldn't manage that. When I saw Amy not fighting for them, it was crushing to me.

DESPITE THE CIRCUMSTANCES

I am very grateful to CPS because they really did have the children's best interest in mind. The children's court-appointed lawyer and his assistant had a huge caseload, but they were always available for the kids. I felt fortunate to have their support.

Three months after having my grandson and granddaughter, CPS in Nevada notified me that my daughter gave birth to a baby boy. He was born six weeks early, weighing three pounds and drug-exposed. He had to be placed in the neonatal intensive care unit for a couple of weeks before going into foster care. During this time, Amy or Scott could have seen the baby, but they chose not to. At this point, the bio-parents still had the opportunity to choose treatment, so they could continue to be parents. Yet, they made no effort. After he was in foster care for a month, CPS brought him to me.

My daughter abandoned my grandson. She didn't choose treatment in order to keep her baby. She just left as if nothing happened. This was a serious offense, which I had no control over. Our family doesn't do things like that. We take care our babies. We don't abandon our tribe. The women in our family are strong fighters; we are not pushovers, and our children come first before any man.

Our family all jumped in to help in any way they could. In fact, I had cousins volunteering to help raise the baby just to help me, knowing that having two children in our home was already a big job. That's how our family is, and Amy knows this. What went wrong?

We couldn't split the kids up. They are the Three Musketeers.

TIME TO GET BUSY

My cousin (whom I grew up with), her husband, my mom, and my son and daughter-in-law were all here to welcome the baby when he arrived. We were all running around trying to set up a nursery and buy things we needed for him. We all fell in love with him. He has been a precious blessing since day one.

The first couple of years are such a blur. Suddenly, I had three small children, one being a newborn. The baby had digestion problems, causing him to vomit several times a day. He didn't sleep well. He twitched while he slept and had other withdrawal symptoms. As a family, we just poured as much love as we could onto him. He is now thriving. It was an adjustment for the two other children because they had gotten used to my undivided attention.

That first year we went through our savings. We had to buy a car that fit three car seats, paint bedrooms, and get new bedroom furniture, clothes, toys, etc. It was actually fun. It made my heart happy to see them excited about all their new things.

There were appointments with doctors, the dentist, and the optometrist, as well as counseling, physical and occupational therapy, court every month, monthly CPS visits. And then, of course, there was the regular cooking, cleaning, and laundry. Life changed that quickly.

The eldest of the three children would have nightmares almost nightly. Both he and his sister would cry for their mother and would ask when she would be back. They would pray for her. The odd thing was they said little about their father. The eldest would have flashbacks about the events he had experienced, which led to breakdowns. I will never forget when his counselor left her position after he'd been seeing her weekly for a year. He had created a bond with her and was very sad at his last appointment. When we got into the car to leave, he said, "Why do people tell you they love you and care about you, then leave you?"

It was a juggling act for me trying to meet the needs of three little broken beings while going through my own grieving process. The loss of my daughter to drugs was like a death to me. I missed her immensely. I wished so much that she was not missing out on these amazing children. They were growing and changing, and it was wonderful to watch every moment.

The following year, it was time for CPS to close the case. The parents were missing in action, as we'd had no word from them in two years. We made the decision to adopt the three grandchildren. The parents had lost their parental rights. It was obvious they weren't coming back. My daughter had picked her path; all I could do was pray for her. My new priority was these three little beings. When the adoption took place, it was a harsh reality at first to think they were no longer Amy's children. I never imagined it would reach this point.

My grandchildren are now my children. They now have present parents. I felt a little insecure at first, knowing that no one can replace your mother. I also didn't want to further alienate my daughter. Actually, there were a lot of mixed feelings that I had to work through. Throwing adoption into the mix was another learning experience. What do the children now call me? Soon enough, organically, they all began to call me Mama. I could see in the eldest, him slowly letting go of the bio-parents because I think he too believed this would not happen on some level. I believe it was the hardest on him because I think he had high hopes his bio-parents would return. In his journal the day before the adoption, he wrote: "Grandma is Going to Be My Mom Tomorrow." As little as he was, he was processing in his own way.

For a long time, they didn't want to play in a different room from where I was. They still have a lot of separation anxiety. The eldest had misplaced resentments toward his little sister; he was responsible for her a lot of the time and blames her for that on an unconscious level. When the baby first arrived, he asked me if he had to take care of him. When I told him no and explained that was my job, he was then happy to have his baby brother join our family. I found it interesting he would think caring for the baby was his responsibility. Both the older kids have post-traumatic stress disorder of abandonment. There are many symptoms related to this disorder, some of which they experience differently. The eldest has some social issues and has a lot of anger to work through. They are all very smart, creative, and funny.

Although it has been almost four years, we are all still adjusting. It is a busy household, but there is so much love. We have gotten into a nice groove. I am grateful each day as I look at the three children, with all their different personalities making them beautiful just the way they are.

CHAPTER TWO

THE SHIFTS

. . . .

Right around the time when the children had been with Scott's sister and I had lost contact with my daughter is when I had a noticeable shift. One of my favorite authors, Dr. Wayne Dyer, passed away during that time. When he passed, I started to reread his books that I had on my bookshelf. They seemed to have a stronger, clearer message this time around. I also started to reread other self-help books on my bookshelf, meditate, and saturate myself with other spiritual things. I noticed my reactions to life and my emotions were more in check. I felt more centered. Had I not been feeding myself in this way, I don't think my old self would have handled things as well as I did and have. The more I grow in my practices, the more shifts I continue to experience along the way. I'm always evolving, just as life is.

Acceptance was one of the big shifts for me. I was in a situation where I hated my life. I hated what my daughter had done, and I hated the father of my grandchildren for what he had done. I was filled with anger because my grandchildren had absent parents and because of all the ramifications my grandchildren had endured and will endure. I wanted to be a grandmother, not a parent. I was continually internally fighting my situation ... having an attitude of how much life sucked and really not wanting to be here. I didn't want to accept my life situation. Maybe I thought if I didn't accept it, all the pain would go away magically, or maybe if I accepted it, then it meant I was giving into something that is horrible. There was constant chaos within me and around me. So, how do I accept that? There was big resistance within me. Nonetheless, wishing, wanting, comparing, reliving the past, projecting into the future, etc. wasn't helping me; it only made things worse.

As I started to understand acceptance better, I realized acceptance is more about accepting the present moment. It's not to say that to put a smile on your face, you have to suck it up and accept anything thrown your way. It is having the understanding that not all things are in one's control. Therefore, if you can change a situation, then, of course, change it. If changing the situation is out of your control, then surrender to what is. Why fight it? There is no sense in fighting it. Fighting what is only adds more misery. As I accepted the current moment, a shift to surrendering to what is took place.

I couldn't change the past. So, going over all the events in my life, why me? Why did this happen? Thinking about all the should haves and could haves and feeling offended and hurt I was pointless. I have come to believe that everything in life has and serves a purpose. Things had unfolded the way they were. No matter how much I try, I can't change the past or this situation. It's impossible.

We tend to want to resist when we are in pain. It's not a natural thing to embrace pain, so we run and hide from it. While it may seem counterintuitive, we also become accustomed to the pain. It's part of our stories, and we identify with it as being who we are. That is why change seems so scary and difficult. So, we stick to the pain because we know it and are used to it. When we are in denial of what is, we don't deal with our emotions. We blame others or the situation. When we are wanting to change a situation or a person, these are all forms of resisting. We get stuck when have that need to control but can't. Our unresolved emotional pain often turns into physical issues. What we resist will persist.

It is freeing to being able to say yes to life rather than opposing it. When you surrender, you detach from the outcome. It may seem a bit scary at first because we are used to wanting to control the outcome. Putting trust into whatever and however life presents itself allows the universal divine intelligence to work on our behalf. When I fought what is, I suffered. When I accepted and surrendered to what is, I was at peace.

All we have is now. Being able to surrender and accept things fully was a very powerful and pivotal moment for me. I no longer feel that my situation is dreadful. I don't feel the need to beg God to change things anymore. Things don't hurt, offend, or bother me so deeply anymore. I no longer take what my daughter did as personal. I no longer ask why. I trust something bigger is at work.

Having a different perspective on life and its challenges took away the expectations that another person or situation would bring me happiness or satisfaction. The ironic thing is the more I accepted and surrendered, the more the external changed for the better. When I lose focus on the present moment, I put my hand to my heart and tell myself that I am okay in this moment and nothing is wrong in the moment. I am reminded to stay present.

FORGIVENESS

Forgiveness came soon after acceptance and surrender. This was another big shift. Everything I ever knew about forgiveness and my perception about forgiveness suddenly changed. Somewhere along the way I had formed the belief that people had to prove they were remorseful in order to be forgiven. I thought even a remorseful person may not deserve forgiveness depending on the offense. I really didn't want to forgive. I had to do some research on forgiveness because I wanted to know why and how is it possible to forgive someone when the transgression seems so grand.

I read where parents forgave when their child was murdered and even forgave when the murderer was not remorseful. I read where people in prison who were wrongly convicted were able to forgive and how people who were abused, raped, and so on were able to forgive. I read how forgiving is liberation. Could I truly give up the anger and the resentments even if I felt so wronged? Could I let go of the hurt and betrayal I felt for my innocent grandchildren who have been subjected to so much?

The dictionary defines the word *forgive* as letting go of resentments, and spiritual leaders claim forgiveness is for the person who is forgiving, not the offender. Forgiving doesn't mean excusing, condoning, or saying it's okay. The other person doesn't even need to know he or she has been forgiven. Actually, forgiving doesn't require further action, other than to let go of hate and resentments and to have the understanding that people only act in the way they know how to at the given time.

In the book *Your Erroneous Zones* by Dr. Wayne Dyer, he shared how all his life he carried around anger, resentments, and abandonment issues because of his father walking out on his mother when he and his brothers were little. As a result, he and his brothers where placed in foster care until his mother was able to reunite them after a number of years. All these negative emotions controlled his life for a very long time. He would wake up sweating in the middle of the night from dreaming about telling is father off. How could he have abandoned them? How could he treat their mother this way? He realized his relationships and life were deeply affected by his father's actions. Later in his life, Dyer found out that his father had died. So, he went to visit his father's grave. He went with the intention to not only curse his father out but to release the negativity he had carried for decades. He stood at the grave and yelled out to his father, cursing and expressing the impact his father had made on him by leaving them.

Somehow, as he was leaving, something told him to go back to the grave. He went back, and as he stood in front of the grave, he decided he would no longer allow what his father had done to control him or define him anymore. Something told him to let it go and forgive. Standing where his father's remains laid, he said to him that he forgave him and from that day forward he would only send him love. Beginning that day, all the hurt, anger, and resentments left him. By forgiving his father's actions, they were no longer a part of him. After that moment, he rarely thought of his father, and when he did, he no longer felt all the negativity. His life dramatically transformed after forgiving and letting go of something that he no longer allowed to define him.

Is everything forgivable? I certainly want forgiveness in my own life. I know I have done things unconsciously. I have hurt people, and I may never know the full impact of that hurt. I have beaten myself up for years for things I am not proud of. So, forgiving myself was first before I could forgive anyone else. In doing so, I had to acknowledge some things before letting go. Our pain becomes so much of who we are that we allow it to define us. We become used to it, so changing it may seem impossible. Having compassion for ourselves spills over to having compassion for others. I have come to find that people only act with the awareness they have at the time. I suddenly saw the things I needed to forgive myself for very clearly and realized how unconscious I had been of them. This helped in being able to forgive my daughter and Scott. They have only acted unconsciously and with the knowledge they had at the time.

In the Bible when Jesus was being crucified, he says, "Father, forgive them, for they do not know what they are doing" (Luke 23:34; New International Version) Those twelve words took on a whole different meaning as I forgave myself, Amy, and Scott. Whatever emotions I felt about the situation were natural. We are humans with human emotions. I allowed myself to feel the hurt, shame, pain, or whatever emotion came up, so I didn't stuff them anymore. I then let it go. Forgiving myself for things in my past was kind of practice for forgiving others. It actually helped me to see there are causalities on both sides of any situation. A new perspective arose, and another layer was lifted. A new level of compassion emerged.

One evening, my husband and I were able to get a sitter and go out to a movie. To my surprise, movie theaters now have bars. We walked over to order a drink, and there was a young guy behind the counter making drinks. He was reading from a recipe book as he went along. When he finished those drinks, he went on to the next couple in front of us. He had to walk to the back to get the ice, and then he went back to his recipe book and proceeded. I kept looking at the time and thinking, *Why is there only one person working? Why don't they have an ice machine up front? Why does the employee have to use a recipe book? Shouldn't he know this by memory? The one time we get to see a movie, and now we're going be late.*

This is a good example of me creating unnecessary anxiety for myself. I have done this self-talk countless times … having expectations of others and believing a situation should be a certain way. This is what was causing me to suffer—not the bartender or the situation. Suddenly, I had an epiphany and started to see myself in this bartender. All at once, I had compassion for him. I was able to put myself in his position. It registered that he was doing his best. I felt bad for judging and carrying on in my head.

When he got to us, he explained the ice machine in front was broken, so he had to go to the back to get ice. He said a couple of employees had called in sick, and although he was not prepared, there was no one else. He appreciated our patience and gave us a discount. This was a major breakthrough for me. It was my thoughts that were creating drama. I could choose to feel inconvenienced or choose to be compassionate. Just by changing my mindset, I was able to witness the peace in that. I stopped thinking, *Why do I have bad luck? Why is this happening?* And when I changed the way I was viewing the situation and my thoughts about it, there was no longer a problem. The more compassion there is, the easier it is to forgive. They go hand and hand. "Forgiveness is the fragrance the violet sheds on the heel that has crushed it". Mark Twain

MINDSET

There are hundreds of books, blogs, and other types of media on the topic of mindset. Mindset techniques are used by athletics, business managers, coaches, leaders of all kinds, employees, and so on. Why? Because they work.

Our beliefs, our thoughts, what we think about ourselves, what we think about our situations, and even our views of the world are just that—thoughts—and thoughts can be changed. If a thought or thoughts are causing suffering, then why not change them? When you change the mind to think positive thoughts, attitude naturally changes. It's always good to have a healthy attitude and positive thoughts because the benefits are endless. I remember in the eighties when affirmations were really big. Even now, I have seen some really beautiful decks of cards with affirmations printed on them. These can be really useful tools when the mind won't stop with the negativity. These types of tools are really good for kids as well because they contain a short positive statement that they can carry with them throughout the day. It's the perfect dose. Sometimes we need these things as reminders to stay positive.

We don't have to be prisoners to old beliefs and the tapes running in our heads. Having a good attitude and positive thoughts will change a person's life; what you put out, you get back. The ability to change my thoughts is a skill I had to develop. It starts with being aware of the thoughts you are thinking. Once I notice a negative thought appear, I replace it with a positive one. Eventually, it becomes second nature. When I had that complaining mentality and wondered, *Why do bad things keep happening to me? Why me?* I only got more of what I complained about. I changed my mindset to think, *What can I learn from this? How can I respond with love versus hate?* That's when the interior changed, resulting in the exterior to change.

The Law of Attraction tells us positive thoughts bring positive experiences and negative thoughts bring negative experiences into a person's life. People and things will show up in a negative way when you think negatively, and the opposite is true when you think positively—more positive people and situations come.

A scripture I really love that speaks to this says, "Finally, brothers and sisters, whatever is true, whatever is noble, whatever is right, whatever is pure, whatever is lovely, whatever is admirable-if anything is excellent or praiseworthy-think about such things" (Phil. 4:8;NIV).

Another one of Dr. Wayne Dyer's books, called *Change Your Thoughts, Change Your Life*, has been really useful in changing negative thought patterns. This is a book that came from a yearlong study that Dyer did on the Tao Te Ching. In each chapter of the book, he gives an explanation of the eighty-one verses that comprised the Tao. I not only learned about the Tao Te Ching, but at the end of each chapter, there is an action piece called "Do the Tao Now," which are daily steps you can incorporate into your life. The steps are to help with changing views and thoughts that block us from living balanced lives. Some of these action steps I do with the children and tweak them according to their ages. For instance, one of the action steps is expressing kindness, love, and appreciation to someone who would be totally surprised. This is in alignment with the twenty-fourth verse where it speaks to showing gratitude for another. I find that the kids love things like this. It bonds us, and we learn together along the way.

The documentary *Heal* (found on Netflix) goes into the science of how our thoughts and beliefs have great impact on how we heal. Three people are followed throughout the documentary. Each has experienced a serious illness, and the program chronicles how changing their belief systems and thoughts contributed to their healing. Science is now telling us that changing our perceptions and beliefs changes our genetic activity. Another important point in the documentary is how trauma affects our health. That is why dealing with trauma and emotional scars are important to work through. Spirituality is another component to healing. Having a trust in a higher power and surrendering to a higher power has been found to be a great contributor to overall health.

I'm finding that even with the children being as small as they are, there is a lot of complaining and negative thinking. I feel it's important for them to start to learn how this type of thinking is a setback, and I promote positive thinking with them whenever I can.

ADDICTION IS A DISEASE

Addiction is defined as a disease by American Medical Association, American Society of Addiction

Medicine, and other medical associations. It is treated the same as diabetes, cancer, and heart disease. Treatment is necessary for these diseases. Addiction is chronic and progressive. It is caused by behavioral, environmental, and biological components. Addiction changes the brain and the behavior in a person. These changes are long term and can persist even after the person has been clean for a while. Although most substance abuse begins with a decision, there is already some type of pain underneath and deeper, underlining reasons for making such a decision. For instance, not living up to their own or others' expectations, wanting to escape reality and the responsibilities in life, the refusal to work through issues and pain, and using drugs, alcohol, a person, food, or whatever to cover up. Some people are more susceptible to addiction than others. However, no one is immune.

As I learned about this disease, I had a big shift in my perception about addiction. It was hard at first for me to understand until I gathered further knowledge. On some level, I felt if I let go of the idea that it is a choice versus a disease, then it would be excusing it in some way. After all, my daughter's choices tore our family apart. However, there are numerous studies on this topic that are worth taking a look at for more understanding of this epidemic.

Unlike other diseases, drugs turn users into lying, conniving, abusive people. Addicts will lose their homes and jobs, steal from their parents, abandon their children, and sell their bodies because once the substance gets hold of them, all logic disappears. It is a baffling, powerful disease. I am not saying in any way that it lessens the responsibility of the addicts because they willfully took the substance to begin with. Plus, there is always the choice to get treatment. But it gives some explanation to the dramatic changes in them and why they do things no one ever thought they would.

In his book *Broken: My Story of Addiction and Redemption*, William C. Moyers gives the reader an inside look from a former addict's perspective. It was good for me to read and see things from the other side. His story is interesting because he came from a family where his parents were quite successful. He went to a prestigious college, enjoyed a great career as a journalist for CNN, and had a wife, children, and a beautiful home on Long Island. His story was another testimony of how parenting and/or being privileged does not make a difference when it comes to addiction. Drugs do not discriminate.

Reading his book and hearing some of his lectures on YouTube helped educate me. In many ways, they altered the way I view addiction and gave me a compassion for the addict that I did not have before. Moyers is the vice president of public affairs for the Hazelden Betty Ford Foundation. Betty Ford Centers have a wonderful children's program, which the eldest attended last spring. It was such amazing experience for both me and the eldest. When you actually hear from the children's own voices about how addiction has affected their lives, you realize how deep addiction is.

Even though we are told that children are resilient, and that is true to some extent, addiction affects the children deeply and profoundly. Hearing it from their own voices and their perspective makes it all the more real. It's an encompassing family and community disease. One of the biggest things is that most children feel the addiction is their fault; they feel they have caused it in some way or they could have stopped it somehow. They tend to feel isolated, like they are the only ones dealing with such issues. Sadly, they are not alone in these feelings. Addiction is not the fault of the children, and they in no way could have stopped it. This program did a good job at teaching this to the children.

I remember the eldest feeling like he could have done something to help his bio-parents stop. He questioned many times why they didn't love him enough to stop or want to be with him. He felt different and isolated from other children. It is still a struggle for him. It was helpful for him to be able to attend this program and be able to express himself. I think it also helped to see that there are other children like him who have similar situations and are going through the same feelings. The program also has a follow-up program and ongoing weekly support group for families.

The effect of the stigma behind addiction is a real eye-opener. Because of the stigma attached to addiction, it is something we don't talk about; therefore, it is not properly addressed, which hinders many things. This type of stigma leads to not enough funding, resources, or emphasis on treatment and recovery. It may even be the reason why many do not choose treatment. Addiction is associated with embarrassment and shame, so we don't talk about the elephant in the room, much less seek help. This kind of thinking perpetuates and oozes out into the community and to the government and lawmakers, making it difficult for treatment, recovery, and family resources.

Society tends to view addiction as some kind a character flaw instead of a real health issue. I know when I looked at treatment centers both times my daughter came to me seeking help it was very discouraging. I couldn't help her by offering her formal treatment. It was impossible for us to come up with thousands or even hundreds of dollars a month, which is what most treatment facilities charge. I understand that now many insurance companies are including addiction treatment in their plans, but what happens when the addict doesn't have insurance?

All these shifts in my thinking were a result of refusing to allow my circumstances to define or dictate my life. I was at point where I didn't want to live my life in that miserable state anymore. The cost was not worth it. My rock bottom was the catalyst to these shifts occurring.

There is a lot of energy put forth when we hold on to grudges and unforgiveness. When we hold on to those people or events that cause us pain or even the unforgiven self, then those things are always a part of our stories. We have to let them go, change our thoughts, and move on. This is the process I went through that shifted things in me and in my life. There is a grieving process I allowed myself to go through. Otherwise, if I didn't allow myself to feel the feelings of grief or if I had tried to stuff them away or feel they are not valid for whatever reason than those unprocessed feelings remain unresolved and would most likely come back to bite me and even create disease (dis-ease). After I acknowledged my feelings and what had happened, cried every tear, and processed through these things, I was able to forgive and let go. Forgiveness had little to do with Amy and Scott. Forgiveness was truly for me. Who would have thought? Most people don't care if you forgive them because most of the time, they are not conscious of what they have done and all the ramifications. So, I didn't need an apology or even for Amy and Scott to be remorseful for what they have done. It's a dramatic change to be free from all of this.

I continually teach my grandchildren that other people's negative actions toward them have nothing to do with them but everything to do with the wrongdoers. It has to do with their level of consciousness. We are conditioned to believe that when the hurt is extreme and the wounds are deep, we have to fight to prove we are right or to make the wrongdoers suffer because we have suffered by their actions. That is just a vicious cycle. When I truly forgave, the need to be right dissipated. The shift in my thoughts actually made me come to feel thankful for these lessons. With the hardest things we go through in life, there is usually something big to learn and a big opportunity to grow.

CHAPTER THREE

THE TOOLS

. . . .

In this chapter, I want to share three tools. They have not only helped with coping, but by consistently practicing these tools, a new life has emerged and continues to develop and grow. My life isn't just about getting by anymore or looking to the next moment or a person to bring me happiness. Instead, my life consists of true peace, acceptance, happiness, and thankfulness.

These tools may resonate with some, and maybe, like me, you even did them at one time and then stopped for some reason. For others, you may find these tools are new to you. These three tools have been useful for my healing and have become part of my daily ritual. I love how I am able to offer these to the children as well. I suggest using these tools to direct you to a path of finding yourself again and finding true peace and happiness.

#1. JOURNALING

When I was a young child, I was always journaling. I would also write short stories and poetry. I loved reading spiritual and personal growth books. When I was in college, I graduated with two minors: one in literature and one in psychology. There has always been something therapeutic about the written word to me, and I find it interesting how the human psyche operates.

When my daughter and the children had gone homeless, I was not only journaling my thoughts and my feelings, but I started to record incidents. This was helpful later when I had to give information to the judge or CPS. Writing things down can be helpful for clarity, and those journals may also be helpful as a reference later on—you just never know.

There are many studies out there proving the power of the pen and paper. At the University of Texas at Austin, psychologist and researcher James Pennebaker found that regular journaling has a positive result on strengthening the immune system and decreasing other physical ailments. Pennebaker believes that writing about stressful events can act as a stress management tool.

When having all these stressful events and many emotions going on, sometimes I didn't know where to turn or what to do. There were times when I just didn't want to talk about my situation anymore because I thought people were getting tired of hearing it. Other times, I found it difficult to communicate at all. This is when I found a lot of relief in my journaling.

There is no right or wrong way to journal. I actually have more than one journal. I have one where I simply write down my thoughts and feelings or perhaps an event I want to remember. I try to do this for at least five minutes a day. Sometimes I set the timer for five minutes and just write whatever comes to mind, not paying attention to spelling or punctuation. It's pretty amazing to see what comes up when I do this.

I have another journal where I place five bullet points each day. I write five things I am grateful for, and many times I will write down more than five items. I do this thankful exercise with the children as well, just in a little different way. We write on a piece of paper something from the day that we are thankful for and put the piece of paper in a mason jar. At the end of the year, we pull out all the pieces of paper, reminisce, and start fresh again for the upcoming year. It's good going over and over the things we are grateful for because it changes a lot of negative energy and is a constant reminder of what is good in our lives. We also talk at some point each evening about one thing from that day that made us laugh or made us happy.

When you write what you are grateful for, there is a change the vibration to a positive one. I see an immediate change in my attitude and in the children too. When I get away from it, believe me, I return to it quickly. The kids are happier when they are focused on gratitude.

Some days in my journaling, I rant. (It's better to get it out on paper than project it onto someone else.) Other times, I write ideas or goals down, but I always make a thankful list. When you are filled with gratitude, things show up in your life. It's about the type of energy being put out. Putting out thankfulness brings more things to be thankful for. The things that are seemingly bad transform when a person is grateful. It changes perception and attitude, and you tend to find the good in everything.

I also have a prayer journal. This is where I write down the names of people who have asked for prayer. It helps to remember and helps to stay connected with these people in a spiritual way in a time of need. Having a prayer journal has helped a lot. When people have asked me to pray for them or someone needs a spiritual lift, I write their names in my journal and visualize them when sending them good energy, love, healing, or whatever it is they seek.

I remember reading many years ago that if you are ever in a situation where you are questioning something, sit with a piece of paper. It has a power behind it. Its's incredible to go back and read my earlier entries and see my growth and even the things I am still struggling with. Journaling can be helpful in so many ways.

I encourage the children to journal as well. I want to be able to help them to learn they have healthy options as they go along in their lives.

#2. MEDITATION AND PRAYER

MEDITATION

Meditation is the backbone to all my practices. Once I began to meditate consistently, my life began evolving with so many life changes and benefits. Meditation will open a person up and gives an awareness you were once blind to. Over the last couple of decades, I have tried different types of meditation. They have all been helpful to me at different times in my life, but somehow, I would always get away from it.

Meditation is one of the first things I returned to in my desperation. I just knew through the chaos that I needed mental space and some mental relief. All the ancient wisdom traditions pointed to the idea that achieving consciousness of the mind and being still and connected to source, higher power, God … is the key to living a more fulfilling and peaceful life. It opens us up to our inner wisdom.

There are so many types of meditations out there. There are sound meditations, guided meditations, breathing, movement, and the list goes on. I have tried guided meditations with the children. However, they like the sound meditations best. Tibetan sound meditations are great. Many of them use singing bowls, which is a beautiful sound. The kids tend to listen to the same one each night before bed. It is called "I am that I am" by Wayne Dyer. The sounds in the meditation come from a discovery Dyer came across through a book called *The Moses Code*. The Moses Code is a result of researching the sounds of the name of God. In the Old Testament, the name of God translated from Hebrew is "I am that I am." In the meditation, there are tuning fork sounds that are used to produce the name of God. It's very soothing. It really relaxes the children, and they sleep soundly and are well rested in the morning.

The main meditation I practice every day is stillness. If that's all I do in a given day, it's enough. Quieting the mind has been a game changer. It gives the mind a chance to declutter and expand. I sometimes will use a guided meditation, but I prefer to just sit in a state of no thinking.

Experts tell us that the mind thinks anywhere between fifty thousand and eighty thousand thoughts per day. Approximately 90 percent of those thoughts are repetitive thoughts. The incessant thinking is the cause of most suffering. We create suffering by thinking the same thoughts over and over. The thoughts are usually filled with drama, assumptions, and negativity. The more often I spend time in silence, the more calmness and peace occurs because it allows for space and for the mind to stop thinking. It's a mental detox of sorts. When you get rid of all that constant chatter, if only for a few minutes, there is peace. An awareness of what you are thinking becomes evident, and soon you become the watcher of your thoughts instead of being your thoughts. Over time, I felt like the space created a bubble around me, protecting me from other people's stuff, their issues, what they think, and my circumstances. As a result, my pain transcended into peace.

By practicing stillness and presence, I was able to overcome a lot of things, anxiety being one of them. Things are able to pass through me more easily, instead of eating away at me. Meditation has given me a way out in a lot of things I felt stuck in.

Claude Debussy, a French composer, has been quoted as saying that it is the space between the notes that makes the music (https://www.azquotes.com/quote/75124). Without the space, it would just be noise. The space is needed for full expression. This is a good description of how meditation works. The space has brought me full expression in the form of shifts, acceptance, surrender, not taking things personally, and forgiveness, and the list goes on and on as I grow. Without these things, the mind would be filled with continuous noise (thoughts) and no growth.

I have read several studies linking meditation to many health benefits. It can lessen anxiety, lower blood pressure, strengthen the immune system, and help with many other physical ailments. There are also a number of studies associating changes in the brain with meditation. I follow several people who have extensively studied the mind-body connection. There is now evidence of neuroscience, epigenetics, and quantum physics in regard to meditation. Deepak Chopra and Dr. Joe Dispenza both have great books, videos, and websites with further information on connections that science has to meditation.

Meditation changes life on many levels. I am able to handle the daily stresses of life, drama, and challenges with greater ease. I'm peaceful more often than not. A tip to maintaining that state throughout the day is to bring awareness to the present moment. When you are aware of the continuous thinking, pause and give the mind some space. I have noticed by consistently practicing this, it's like strengthening a muscle; it gets easier to access with more practice.

The more space the mind has, the more life flows. You don't feel in opposition to life but welcome it.

There are several guided meditations that can be found on YouTube and vary in time. I decide which meditation to use to guide me based on the amount of time I have and what I feel I need. It doesn't have to take long, and many of the meditations I use are no longer than thirty minutes. Some are as little as twelve minutes. The important thing is to give the mind a break. The great thing about practicing presence and stillness is it can be done anytime and anywhere.

Something very different I have found from when I first learned meditation decades ago is that it is not necessary to sit or breathe a certain way, and it doesn't need to take hours to attain the benefits. I have also found that the mind can be very noisy at times, and instead of fighting the mind trying to achieve the perfect state, I allow it to be. I just let the thoughts be and don't engage in them, and they soon float away. There is a peacefulness that comes when there is no longer condemning or fighting oneself.

PRAYER

Once in the eighties and another time in the nineties, I read the Bible from front to back, which took a year each time. I have also studied various religions and have studied the book *A Course in Miracles*. Most spiritual texts and religions point to prayer and the belief in God, source, the universe, or higher power as a significant part to a fulfilled life. Spending time in silence created in me a deeper connection to God, and my prayer life changed. The space in meditation produces a type of oneness with source. Because of this, many of my prayers are those of gratitude. I am able to see my blessings now instead of taking them for granted. I no longer feel the need to beg God to change my daughter or my situation. I don't wish anymore for things to be the way they used to be or how they are supposed to be. I have come to trust that whatever comes is always for a higher good even if it appears not to be.

Elisabeth Kübler-Ross, a medical doctor whose faith in prayer is legendary, says, "You will not grow if you sit in a beautiful flower garden, but you will grow if you are sick, if you are in pain, if you experience losses, and if you do not put your head in the sand, but take the pain as a gift to you with a very, very specific purpose." The pain from watching our adult children go down the path of drugs and all that goes with that, as well as witnessing the suffering of our grandchildren (through no fault of their own), can be unbearable. However, if we trust there is a specific purpose for all involved, believe there are no mistakes, and let go of the outcome, that's when prayer is in the works.

There can be big changes in the mind the more you become aware of your thoughts. Being aware is the beginning of being able to change your thoughts about life. When you are connected and grounded, you grow a deep trust that whatever life throws your way, there is a knowing that there is a greater purpose. I don't need to know all the answers. I just allow for things to flow and not fight myself or things anymore. When staying in the present moment, you enjoy the now—the current moment—which is all we really have. When you go within, you find your true essence, which is love and where God resides. "Be still and know that I am God" (Ps. 46:10; NIV).

An important book that goes into depth on stillness, being present, and quieting the mind is *The Power of Now* by Eckhart Tolle. In it, he says, "Realize deeply that the present moment is all you have. Make the NOW the primary focus of your life." He also says, "When you surrender to what is and so become fully present, the past ceases to have any power. You do not need it any more. Presence is the key. The Now is the key. How will I know when I have surrendered? When you no longer have to ask the question."

This is a book I have read over and over. Each time I read it, I get a deeper understanding. Tolle has a website with many resources, from courses to meditations and such. I was able to take one of the courses called "Becoming a Teacher of Presence," and this past year I enrolled in a six-month course he offers through his School of Awakening. I received a scholarship, so I was able to have this experience when I might not have been able to otherwise. Saying the six-month course changed my life is an understatement. Learning how to access the state of consciousness has been liberating and life changing.

#3. TAPPING—EFT

Tapping is another tool that can be used on yourself and on the children. It can bring a lot of relief to emotional baggage and physical pain. Tapping, also known as EFT (Emotional Freedom Technique) is a wonderful tool with fairly instant results. It is similar to acupuncture. Acupuncture is an ancient Chinese medical technique where needles are placed along the meridians to help clear up energy. Our bodies are made of energy, so when there is stuck energy, we can experience physical and mental pain.

The good things about tapping are that it is free, it can be done at home, and you use your fingertips instead of needles. I can't remember how I was introduced to tapping, but I experimented first with myself, and when I saw how quickly I got results, I introduced it to the children. The results with the children have been amazing. For example, once when the eldest had a temper tantrum and I first used tapping with him, I saw his body relax and saw his attitude change almost immediately. I felt it empowered him in a way. He will even ask me if we can tap when he is feeling any uneasiness.

I have read many accounts where tapping has helped children with bed-wetting, school (both academically and socially), sport performance, depression, obsessive-compulsive disorder, trauma, and a number of other ailments. This is true for adults as well.

When you start to tap, you rate the intensity of the issue on a scale of zero to ten and then repeat the process until the intensity reaches zero. With tapping, there are statements that are made about the problem as you tap. The premise is you identify the feeling and say a statement acknowledging that feeling. Then a positive statement follows. For instance, if my eldest is having a tantrum, while tapping, he might say something like this: "Even though I am angry, I deeply love and accept myself." Tapping on the acupuncture points and repeating the statement in combination was very powerful from the first time I used this method with both the older children.

Because the kids now know the routine, when they are in the midst of some type of stressful situation, I sometimes will just start tapping without any statement. Automatically, they just following along tapping, and change soon follows.

The eight tapping points are the eyebrow, side of the eye, under the eye, under the nose, chin, collarbone, underarm, and top of the head. Tapping these areas has been proven to make changes in the nervous system and clear blocks.

There is a children's book called, *Gorilla Thumps and Bear Hugs: A Tapping Solution Children's Story* by Alex Ortner, which I read to the children. It is actually one of their favorite books, and they ask me to read it often. It teaches tapping techniques in a story relatable to children. Ortner and his siblings own a company called The Tapping Solution; the website is filled with information on tapping and the many ways it can be used. Another great resource on tapping is EFT Universe. The founder is Dawson Church, PhD; he has two books out that are great reads, *Mind to Matter* and *The Genie in Your Genes*, which I highly recommend. His EFT Universe offers workshops, courses, and certification on tapping.

Tapping can be used for optimal health, pain management, business, finances, relationships, weight loss, depression, forgiveness, addiction, anxiety, post-traumatic stress disorder, and manifestation. Many psychotherapists and counselors have now added EFT as part of the therapy they offer.

I have used tapping for many issues. In the beginning, when I would have very bad anxiety attacks, I used EFT and felt relief almost right away. The good thing is that I rarely experience anxiety anymore. It has mainly allowed me to work through the grief and negative emotions I was carrying around or that will come up when triggered. A lot of times we feel if we ignore our feelings, they will go away or we feel that what we are feelings is not warranted or not worth dealing with. However, when we don't acknowledge our feelings, they don't go away. The negative emotions stay stuck in our bodies. We are energy, so when we are stuck, we can't move easily. A lot of times, it's difficult to identify all the emotions you are dealing with. You might think you are angry, but as you tap, you may find there are other emotions that come up. As a result, you are able to find the true underling emotion, and then you can work on that. The goal is to clear all the negative stuff that is holding you back.

Another thing I have found useful is called toe tapping. I learned this a number of years ago in a yoga class I was attending. It's an exercise where you lay on your back and tap your two big toes together for five to ten minutes. It helps with moving circulation around and getting the flow of energy moving. I notice the children sleep much better after doing this, especially after an emotional type of day.

There are tapping videos on YouTube that you can follow along with. Search *tapping* or *EFT* and whatever issue you want to get rid of, and you will find there are many videos. There is also a good chance of finding a therapist who includes this in their therapy.

EFT is another tool to add to your toolbox. Some things work for some and not for others. It's always worth a try.

CHAPTER FOUR

THE JOURNEY

. . . .

Life is a never-ending journey. Life is also unpredictable. It is easy to forget this because we grow attachments to possessions and people. We have conditioning that has told us things need to be a certain way in order to be happy. There is the notion still today that we are supposed to go to college, choose a career, get married, buy a home, and have children, and that is the key to happiness. If these things don't happen, in that order nonetheless, then there is this idea that something is wrong with us or that something went wrong along the way. This creates a separation and unnecessary labeling, and we all get caught up in it. By having an open mind and the willingness to do whatever it takes to be at peace, I was led to the books I read, the investigation I did, and the tools I have shared that produced healing in me. It starts with an openness and willingness, but a commitment is needed to yourself daily because life is so unpredictable and will take you away if you are not centered. You have to stay grounded in order to weather the storms.

For more than thirty years, I was preparing for the challenge of my life. I just didn't know it. It is no accident that for decades I studied different forms of spirituality and personal growth. It wasn't until I was in complete misery and hit my rock bottom that it all started to click and kick in. Everything I had learned was needed when I was ready for change. Before, it was like a temporary spiritual high, and because I had no real commitment to continue growing spiritually, it didn't last. This time around, I remained open and committed, and things started happening and continue to happen. I was pointed in a direction of healing by the past and future leaders I have mentioned throughout the book. Their expertise and teachings led me to where I am today, which is at peace.

All the studying and research I have done over the years were building blocks. When I hit my rock bottom, it was all there; I just needed to return to it. One thing led to another, and I discovered that not only was all the learning in my past right there in the background but so was I—my lost self. By adding new learning, it supported me through one of the hardest things to deal with in life. Engulfed in my pain, I lost myself. Everything we need is inside of each and every one of us; we just forget and are taken away by life's troubles. It's just as Glinda the Good Witch from *The Wizard of Oz* said: "You've always had the power, my dear. You just had to learn it yourself."

We are all a part of something bigger. When we connect to that—the bigger picture, the universe, God, source—then our meaning for existence and other things shifts. There is no difference in the internal essence that we all have in common. We may look different on the outside, but we are all essentially the same. Understanding this levels the playing field; it creates a oneness, and things like labeling and judging vanish. Forgiveness, compassion, and love emerge. People usually change when they have had enough. As the Tao Te Ching states, "When the student is ready, the teacher will appear."

Things are not always fully revealed to us, and especially during hard times, this is where we need to learn to trust all things in good time and all things for our higher purpose. When we have the mindset that our struggles and challenges are our teachers instead of viewing those things as some kind of curse or something personal, then we are able learn and move through things more easily. We gain a kind of patience and trust—if not this time, then another time or not at all—but the trust is knowing that even though we don't see it or understand it, it is part of a bigger plan. It's a trust and the giving away of something we can't control.

When we experience trauma of any kind, it can immobilize us for many years and sometimes for our entire lives. Our minds stay stuck with the thoughts of the situation, and then we are unable to function and move through life effectively and happily. When our minds are continually going over what went wrong, how painful it all was/is, and how horrible the future will be because of it and we let others' advice rule over our own intuition, it throws us off course and leads to more pain. When we stop all this and use our minds for what they are needed for instead of letting the mind/thoughts control us, we are able trust our instincts because we aren't clogged up.

There is a trusting that things will unfold the way they are supposed to, and we are okay with that. That's not to say we kick back and do nothing. It's important to take action when possible. However, a lot of it is just trusting and going with the flow of things. When a challenge arises, instead of getting caught up in all the negative, I ask myself: *What am I supposed to learn from this?* I find there is actually lot to learn in any given challenge.

I now believe when we're thrown off the path by our decisions or the choices of others, there is always a lesson involved. My responsibility to myself is to get back on my path and learn from any given situation for my higher good. We can't wait for someone to help us or to save us, much like our adult addicts. We need to be our own advocates because no one else will be. Going within each day and finding God and myself there is how I stay in alignment. When I'm in alignment, shifts occur, and things come and flow rhythmically.

When I changed my way of thinking, it made it easier to let go of attachments—both to people and how things should be. People and the external events are fleeting; that's just how life is. Nothing lasts forever. Therefore, people and events have nothing to do with happiness. Our job is to stay centered, so we are not sent off to some state of oblivion when life events happen.

The shifts I made changed the person I once was. I was once oversensitive. I overreacted continually, took things personally, struggled with depression, and really didn't like life. I was repeatedly seeking for something outside of me, hoping, expecting, wanting, and looking to the next moment to make me happy. Something always felt like it was missing, and I could never figure it out. The things I once battled, resisted, and/or tolerated transformed when I truly let go. I began to value who I am and what deserved my time, energy, and focus. It's a complete illusion to think if this or that happens, *then* I will be happy and complete. It never works or lasts that way for long. What is important is already inside us and here now—not in the next moment or by the conditions of someone else. We just need to remember that.

The tools I share are how I fill myself up daily. It is important for my cup to be full. After all, I can't raise these three small children being half empty or empty. We can't give when we are running on empty. It's not easy going 24/7, and it is easy to forget that and neglect ourselves, which brings me to self-care.

SELF-CARE

I happen to think that self-care and self-love are interchangeable. I'm all about taking long, hot baths, getting a massage, getting my nails or hair done, and napping. All those things are great ideas and are important. My daily tools/rituals are also a form of self-care. Feeling that we deserve these things is another story. According to the Oxford dictionary, *self-love* means: "regard for one's own well-being and happiness (chiefly considered as a desirable rather than narcissistic characteristic)." So, yes, not in an arrogant way that creates separation or competition, but in a way that is nurturing to our own selves.

I know it's really hard to leave behind that feeling of being responsible in some way for our adult children's choices or having a strong inclination to want to fix things for them. It's ingrained in us as parents. When we feel like we have failed, it creates a type of low self-esteem and self-loathing. As life would have it, things don't go well often; that is just the way life is with its ups and downs. A part of self-love is to see where true responsibility lies, rather than beating ourselves up for something that is truly not our fault or is out of our control.

When we love ourselves, we understand we are only responsible for our own lives, and that is truthfully our only responsibility in the long run. The more self-love we have, the more we are able to make better decisions. The decisions then come from love and not fear. Self-love helps us stay grounded, and our intuition becomes clearer and sharper. There is a knowing within opposed to being tossed around and listening to what others or the world tells us. We stop giving our power away when we love ourselves. We are able to create healthy boundaries.

Love is essentially who we all are. We need to remember that when we lose focus. It's inside there—in each and every one of us—since the day we came into existence. When we tap in to loving ourselves, we are able to forgive, have more compassion, and give genuine love because we accept and love ourselves for who we are. In turn, we are able to love and accept others for who they are as well. When we care less about what others think, then we don't take things as personally. In *The Four Agreements*, a book based on Toltec knowledge by Don Miguel Ruiz, the second agreement is, "Don't take anything personal." I had been told by Amy on many occasions how things were my fault, I wasn't good enough, I was making it about me, I was crazy, and other hateful things. It made me question myself, what I did wrong, what I could have done differently, and so on. The number one thing I hear from parents of adult addicts is the blame the addict projects upon them. It's hard not to take it personally. Even though you may know addicts will manipulate, blame, accuse, and want others to suffer along with them, you can't help but take it personally.

Then we have society and all the programing, telling us that our children (good, bad, successful, or not) are a result of our parenting. So, how could any parent not take it personally or not feel responsible in some way? In *The Four Agreements*, it explains further how others' opinions are about that person. It is not about the receiver. When we take on others' opinions, we take on their garbage. In actuality, our adult children's actions are not about the parents. We are the punching bags. The blame and insults are about the addict. We can make the choice to take on their garbage or let it pass right on through. This is the type of advice we give people we care about, yet we rarely apply this to ourselves. The more I have practiced self-love, the easier it is to speak my truth, stay quite when needed, and not place so much value on what others think, say, or do.

Another aspect to keeping one's cup full is keeping it free of clutter. We have to remember that we can't give from a half-empty or dry cup, but we also can't give from one filled with junk. When we love ourselves, we become more aware of what we put in our bodies and what and whom we surround ourselves with—from the food we put in our mouths to the programs and movies we watch to the overindulgences we partake in to the feeding into the desire of "I want." When we relinquish coming from a place of "I want" and come from a place of abundance, that is what we get more of. What comes out of our mouths is less complaining, less judging, and less reactiveness to life. Our daily actions change dramatically, and good things follow.

Each Sunday, I tune into *Super Soul Sunday*. It's a program Oprah hosts on the Oprah Winfrey Network. In each show, she interviews authors, spiritual teachers, and just plain inspiring human beings. It is always filled with heart-provoking features. By constantly reading spiritual and uplifting books, watching uplifting movies and programs, and listening to podcasts and personal growth lectures, I am fed in a positive way. It is not always easy finding the time to read, so sometimes it is only a chapter here and there or an audiobook while cleaning. If it wasn't from all the reading I have done, I would never have received such beautiful messages from strong pioneers, leaders, and professionals who were passionate enough to share with the world. And by watching and listening to things that fill me up, it keeps me in line for caring and loving myself.

A big part of loving ourselves is to do what it takes to be happy and at peace. Everyone is different and at different stages, and sometimes this means taking small steps. Small steps lead to bigger steps and so on, and this keeps a person anchored. And when anchored, you figure out what you need and what works for you.

LOVE

I know at times we feel the true emotional feeling of hate. We hate our lives or hate what our adult addicts have become. We hate seeing our children suffer and hate the pain they have caused. We hate that we have to see our grandchildren struggle. We hate that we can't help or change the situation. We could even go on to say that we hate discrimination, we hate drugs, we hate injustice, and we hate any kind of destruction. We would not be human if we did not experience this gut-wrenching hate for such things. However, hate does not change a thing. It only adds to an already negative situation.

When we replace love with hate, fear diminishes, and we actually feel lighter because we are not carrying around the heavy burden of hate. We don't have to love these things, but we don't have to hate them either. When we remember that each person is inheritably a loving presence, we began to see the distinction between spirit and form, thus creating a thread of love. We are able to love more freely when we are not stuck in our old ways of thinking and doing that have not worked anyway and instead have just made us feel weighed down and yucky.

When I feel hate creeping up toward anyone or anything, I ask myself how I can replace it with love. Many times, it is the same answer, which is to stay in my lane and let others stay in their lanes. If it is a situation I can change, I will try my best, but if I can't and it is out of my control, then the loving thing may be to stay silent or stay away. How does hate help or change it? Hate never helps anything. There is a lot of mental energy wasted in negative emotions. If hate is overwhelming—let's say because of the impossible addict—then turn the focus to loving others.

Practicing random acts of kindness cultivates more love. I often go through my closets and give away things that are practically new and are just sitting there not being used. It's a good way to practice not being attached to material things, letting go, and giving to someone in need. Giving without expecting anything in return is good way to bring more love into your life. The more love there is, the less room there is for hate of any kind.

The poet Rabindranath Tagore wrote, "God loves to see in me, not his servant, but himself who serves all." When we come from a place of love, we heal ourselves and others. Of course, we are not going to love all things, but just like fear, disappointment, or sadness, any and all human emotions that hold us back should be worked through, so those emotions are not left stuck in the body creating turmoil. Identifying what is underneath the hate and allowing those feeling to surface and dealing with them instead of suppressing them opens a person up to more love.

Gratitude is yet another way to develop more love. When we start to notice what is good in our lives, there is an awareness that increases. We notice things we once overlooked or took for granted. Being grateful generates a climate of positivity and loving feelings. You feel more alive and motivated because you bring forth the good and push out the bad. When you extend love and positive thoughts out, you begin to react in more loving ways. Another way to bring more love into the world is by asking: How may I serve?

IT'S A SOCIAL ISSUE

I have heard many people's stories. We are all at different places with our addicts. The emotions we go through are the same. Some have more than one adult addict child, some are raising both grandchildren and great-grandchildren, and others, without raising the grandchildren, are watching the adult addicts destroy their lives and abandon their children. Some have even buried their children. There is also incarceration, foster care, mental illness, and much more.

This is a social issue that impacts many individuals. There are no easy answers. There is an organization called The Faces and Voices of Recovery. They are promoters of public policy, stigma reduction, resources, family recovery advocacy, and much more. You can find their policy agenda on their website (https//facesandvoicesofrecovery.org). Their belief is that investing in long-term recovery will benefit the economy by providing a stronger support system, thus reducing the burden of what we see today. Addiction is not only a family problem but, in fact, goes far and beyond that.

In this life, I have come to find that we don't always get what we want, what we pray for, or what we wish for, and that can hurt, be disappointing, bring deep sadness, and feel like a living hell. As I said before, all those very real feelings need to be worked through. We don't have to walk around with all those stuck negative emotions that keep us from moving forward. Our situations do not need to define us; they are not who we are, and this does not have to be the end of our stories. Your situation can actually be the beginning of a new start if you want it to be.

I remember feeling so busy that the thought of adding one more thing to my life seemed impossible. Now, loving and caring for myself and doing my daily routines doesn't feel like I am adding another thing to my already busy life. In fact, I long and look forward to doing my journaling, meditating, and tapping. As Lao Tzu said, "The journey of a thousand miles begins with one step at a time."

I still feel that pull and tug from time to time. It's part of being a parent. When I saw that my daughter was not interested in doing whatever it takes to be clean and live a life she is worthy of, I had to face my fears, my heartache, and my pain and accept that. However, I am willing to do whatever it takes to live a life I am worthy of. We are on different paths. I understand that now. The tools I do each day—and I sometimes do them several times a day—are what have kept me grounded. By being grounded, I am able to not be tossed around when the winds come. I am not easily taken away. I remind myself I can change my thoughts and perception at any time, and when I do, the stress decreases.

A Course in Miracles describes a change in perception as being a miracle. It's a miracle because the blocks, the fear, the guilt, etc. are removed. A veil is taken off. It's not that anything externally changes. The miracle is the change in perception ... The change is internal. When things change internally, things feel and look different. There is an awareness and aliveness. I started to notice the different types of trees in my neighborhood and all the details of each tree. The mountains looked closer, more expansive, and the colors seemed more vivid. It was like having a new, fresh pair of lenses.

The more and more I am able to stay in the present moment, the less distracted I am with my loss. I can't say enough about practicing silence and being present. Being present in the moment brings a consciousness and joy to whatever I am doing in the current moment. When we place attention in the now, we are not bombarded with all the other stuff like the continuous chatter in our heads and people and their stuff. When we understand the now is all we have and our attention is on that, life is actually enjoyable. You are not looking to the next moment to bring you joy because you are already experiencing it in that moment.

Being in silence or any type of meditation opens up the heart and frees the mind, so accepting things comes easily. There is an awareness that brings consciousness, and through the conscious awareness, life changes. There is less reactiveness. As awareness grows, things that once consumed our lives become weakened. Things start to flow versus being stuck and stagnate. Our true selves emerge, and there is a sense of true meaning and purpose. When we stop trying to find ourselves in others or in the external world, we don't have to try so hard. Things transform in an organic way.

Paradoxically, the more presence you bring into your life, the more things show up. People and things show up in unexpected ways. Synchronicities and signs appear, and the amazing thing is that you will actually notice them. Carl Jung's work on synchronicity has said there is a meaning in the apparent coincidences that show up in our lives. For instance, when I wanted to learn more about living a conscious life and expand on what I was learning, The School of Awakening showed up. As I read through the description of the six-month course, there were bullet points detailing what would be presented. It was exactly what I wanted. I scrolled down to the bottom and saw the cost and thought, *Well, that's a bummer. I have formula, diapers, and other kid things I need to buy.* Lo and behold, underneath the cost a little farther down was a button to click to apply for a scholarship. And guess what? I received one. I am consistently receiving things I need without much effort; they just flow to me.

PARENTING

So much has changed in thirty years in regard to raising children. There are numerous books out there on parenting. There is a big difference in parenting the second time around, and those differences are even more profound when dealing with traumatized children or children born exposed to drugs.

I remember when I had my first two children, who are now adults. I read every parenting book I could. I had no clue what parenting entailed. When I raised my first two children, I was heavily involved in a Christian church, so I used a combination of Christian values with some of what I found in my readings on the most effective ways to parent.

Flash forward thirty years. Suddenly, we adopt our three grandchildren, and parenting is facing us straight on again. There is a whole new set of issues we are unexpectedly confronted with. We look at these children whom we love with all our hearts, and we see their psychological, emotional, and spiritual needs. Then we look at ourselves and wonder how we can meet this challenge with some success.

On top of this, because of our unique situation, we are going through our own stuff. It's a balancing act for sure. When I was parenting the first time around, I was in my twenties, and now I am in my fifties. The energy and spunk I had back then has calmed quite a bit. At first, it made me wonder about my abilities. I was concerned about the stigma of being an older parent and how it would affect the children in their school years. One of the first things I did was put the kids into counseling. It helped that we did everything through the courts and CPS because the children were given Medicaid for their medical needs. Otherwise, it would have been impossible with the costs involved in medical care.

I got my eldest in the Betty Ford children's program. (The other two were not old enough for the program.) I delved into everything and anything I could to find resources and help. As I went along, I became more aware of the biggest difference in my adult children and my new set of children, which is trauma. Trauma encompasses so much. It's deep and disrupts normal daily functioning. Traumatized brains are developed differently. We can't parent children with trauma the same way. It doesn't work that way because there are too many intricacies.

We are faced with so many issues, and it is hard to know where to begin. Again, this is yet another opportunity to reconnect to our true selves. We find answers when we are centered. I found that by doing my own work and finding myself again, a lot of my concerns worked themselves out. It is not like magic, where it all just happens. I am still busy every minute of every day, so I am working it. At the same time, by returning to my authentic self, I am able to better tune in to what the children's needs are and how to go about it. Like I said earlier, the right people and the right opportunities appear. When we live a more conscious life, we are able to project that onto our children and onto the world. It gives others the opportunity and our children the chance of becoming conscious adults.

By being present in our daily lives, we build a deeper connection with our children, which is valuable. If we do all the right things or even if we mess up, it doesn't really matter as much when there is a deep connection with our children. There are hundreds of ways to approach raising children. It can be confusing when we start grasping and trying to find solutions. There are just as many solutions as there are approaches. What I do know is that through the tools I have learned, I have been able to include the children in the journaling, meditation, and tapping, which also creates a connection and bond. Connection and bonding can get people through a lot together. I am not only leading by example, but it provides them with concrete tools to help them navigate through their own lives as they grow.

In Closing ...

As complicated as this all is, there is also a simplicity component. When we are able to live lives where we feel grounded and at peace, then complications are able to be recognized and dealt with. It's a matter of deciding peace over chaos.

I love my daughter with all my heart. I miss who she once was. I feel sad knowing she has missed out on so much. The three children are all so very unique. They are growing and changing. She doesn't know them. They don't know her. When I send her love and healing, it's not for me but for her. I know it's her path, her choices, and in her own time, and I also know that it may never be. I am still thankful from what I have learned from her. I am honored to have the opportunity to adopt, love, and care for my grandchildren who are now my children. They teach me so many things on a daily basis. They bring joy and make me laugh every day. Knowing they are a part of my life and I am part of theirs joined in this way brings so much happiness and gratitude.

I want to thank you for reading this book, and I hope there is something of value each and every reader can take away. Remember who you are and live authentically. I want to end with this beautiful poem, "Remember". It is written Joy Harjo. She is the first Native American US Poet Laureate.

Remember

Remember the sky that you were born under, know each of the star's stories.

Remember the moon, know who she is.

Remember the sun's birth at dawn, that is the strongest point of time. Remember sundown and the giving away to night.

Remember your birth, how your mother struggled to give you form and breath. You are evidence of her life, her mother's, and hers. Remember your father. He is your life, also. Remember the earth whose skin you are: red earth, black earth, yellow earth, white earth brown earth, we are earth.

Remember the plants, trees, animal life who all have their tribes, their families, their histories, too. Talk to them, listen to them. They are alive poems.

Remember the wind. Remember her voice. She knows the origin of this universe.

Remember you are all people and all people are you.

Remember all is in motion, is growing, is you. Remember language comes from this. Remember the dance language is, that life is. Remember

(readpoetry.com)

ABOUT THE AUTHOR

Tabitha Sage holds a Bachelor's degree from the University of Vermont. She has an extensive background in spiritual and religious fields of study but it took a real-life lesson of climbing from the depths of despair for it to all kick in and for life to start working again.

For the last two and half decades, she has been a student of the teachings of Dr. Wayne Dyer. She has completed certified coursework through Eckhart Tolle's School of Awakening along with the completion of "Becoming a Teacher of Presence" curriculum. There are many other personal growth courses she has studied over the past 30 years that have contributed to her growth and healing.

Tabitha turned her devastating journey, coupled with her extensive spiritual studies to provide readers loving and supportive steps towards their own healing and awakening for a better life, not just for one's own self but for the entire family.

RESOURCES

Inspiring Meditations

Alan Watts: Guided Meditation -https://youtu.be/ jPpUNAFHgxM

Darshan Atmosphere: What Is Meditation – https:// youtu.be/Ot23i24qQqE

Deepak Chopra's: Go-To 3-minute Mediation -https://youtu.be/4BsOqUB3BHQ

Eckhart Tolle: Stillness Meditation – https://youtu. be/fWEX3SRX7Ro

Guided Meditation by Gregg Brandon, June 2018 – https//youtu.be/T8aelrtzaSo

I am that I am by Wayne Dyer – https//youtu.be/ HiTtEQX2o8

Meditations for a Miraculous Life (Money Meditation) – Marianne Williamson – https://LIKRuJOET7s

Who Am I? Guided Meditation with Kim Eng – https://youtu.be/Qk5dlmyIOZk

Inspiring Books

A New Earth by Eckhart Tolle

A Return to Love: Reflections on the Principles of A Course in Miracles by Marianne Williamson

Becoming Supernatural by Dr. Joe Dispenza

Broken: My Story of Addiction and Redemption by William Cope Moyers

Change Your Thoughts, Change Your Life by Wayne Dyer

Dying to Be Me by Anita Moorjani

Gorilla Thumps and Bear Hugs: A Tapping Solution Children's Story by Alex Ortner

Mind to Matter by Dawson Church

Now What? An Insider's Guide to Addiction and Recovery by William Cope Moyers

She Had Some Horses by Joy Harjo

The Bible (I like the New International Version.)

The Book of Secrets by Deepak Chopra

The Four Agreements: A Practical Guide to Personal Freedom by Don Miguel Ruiz

The Isaiah Effect by Gregg Braden

The Power of Now by Eckhart Tolle

The Tapping Solution for Parents, Children and Teenagers by Nick Ortner

The Torah

You Can Heal Your Life by Louise Hay

Your Erroneous Zones by Wayne Dyer

Inspiring Weekly Television Show

Super Soul Sunday, Oprah Winfrey Network (on Sundays)

Inspiring Movies and Documentaries

Awake: The Life of Yoganda (The whole movie can be found on YouTube)

Heal, Netflix (healdocumentary.com)

Ram Dass, Going Home, Netflix

The Shift, Wayne Dyer (The whole movie can be found on YouTube)

Inspiring/Informative Websites

deepakchopra.com

djoedispenza.com

eckharttolle.com

eftuniverse.com

thetappingsolution.com

Printed in the United States
By Bookmasters